I Can Do All Things

21 Day Devotional for People with Disabilities

Inspiring examples of God's blessings

By Francine Hilliard Bell

I Can Do All Things

A 21 Day Devotional for People with Disabilities

By Francine Hilliard Bell

Copyright 2012

DEDICATIONS

To my parents, the late George & Evelyn Hilliard who had 20 children including two with special needs. Following my father's death, my Mother struggled, but finished raising the remaining seven younger children on her own with Gods help. My Mom's strong faith carried us through and helped me become the woman I am today. She was the perfect Mother. Throughout my many trips to the doctor, the hospital, surgery, physical therapy, most of the time it was just her, me and God. Those one on one moments with her in one waiting room after another are treasured memories.

To my Brothers and Sisters and my beautiful daughter Hilary, thank you for using your experience with me to help you as you encounter people with disabilities. To my granddaughters Sarah and NaSyah, you are truly a blessing to my life.

To all my friends and others living with a disability this book is for you.

Dear Reader,

Thank you for taking time to read this devotional. I am not a Bible scholar or an ordained minister but I am a student of God's word. I don't assume to know everything about anything. I only know what God has done for me and wanted to share it with you. If one person is helped, encouraged, strengthened, or comforted, then this book was worth the effort.

May God's blessing be on you as you read it along with your Bible.

To God be the Glory

Francine H. Bell, Author

Bible Versions Quoted:

New International Version

The New Living Translation

Other references from:

BibleGateway.com

WebMD.com

eHow Health (Internet)

The Hunchback of Notre Dame by Victor Hugo (1831)

Table of Contents

God Will Give You Things to Do – Day 1

Can Do Spirit – Day 2

Persevering in the Midst of
Uncontrollable Circumstances – Day 3

The Purpose God Sees in Us – Day 4

The Journey… Through Weakness and Into Strength – Day 5

ADA… In God's Plan – Day 6

The Cure All for All – Day 7

God Sees the Heart – Day 8

Cracks in the Sidewalk – Day 9

Ice Chips – Day 10

Your Walk – Day 11

Never Without the Spirit Within – Day 12

A Special Child for Special Needs – Day 13

Don't Leave Home Without Him – Day 14

The Presence of God – Day 15

A Question of Faith – Day 16

Where Is The Thanks – Day 17

Waiting in Faith – Day 18

I Shall Trust and Not Worry - Day 19

You Need My Help – Day 20

God Sees Us – Day 21

God Will Give You Things To Do – Day 1

"Lord, if it's you," Peter replied, "tell me to come to you on the water." "Come," he said. Then Peter got down out of the boat, walked on the water and came toward Jesus. But when he saw the wind, he was afraid and, beginning to sink, cried out, "Lord, save me! Immediately Jesus reached out his hand and caught him. "You of little faith," he said, "why did you doubt?" (Matthew 14:28-31)

"And we know that God causes everything to work together for the good of those who love God and are called according to His purpose for them." (Romans 8:28)

Do you realize that God has been watching you since before you were born? He has things planned for you that may seem impossible to imagine. In my case, he worked through my Mother who had remarkable faith, though I didn't realize it at the time. One day she really sensed my frustration when I went so far as to tell her that I wished I were dead. Her words to me "Someday God will give you things to do, so that what you can't do won't matter." I thought she was just being motherly and doing her motherly thing. I was wrong.

Apart from your disability, what is going on in your life right now that you can point to and say that it has you extremely busy; so busy that when you're engrossed in it, you don't think about your disability. Could it be taking care of your family, working on your job, serving in your church or community, or learning a new skill? For me it's helping my daughter care for my grandchildren, writing this devotional, working on my job and a host of other projects.

We have to keep our focus on Jesus and the work he's given us to do. Peter walked on water, but when he took his eyes off Jesus, he became frightened of his circumstances and began to sink. Allow God to take your disability away from being the focus of your life. He can make it sit in the shadow of his blessings and give you a life where disability is no longer the monster that dominates your every waking hour. God will give you things to do and what you can't do will no longer matter.

Prayer: *Dear God, Thank you that what I can't do with my body is no longer a constant issue. Thank you that I am here and can give you all the praise, honor, and glory. When my disability becomes my main focal point, draw my attention back to you. Remind me of the countless blessings you've given me and that your grace is sufficient.*

Can Do Spirit – Day 2

"I can do everything with the help of Christ who gives me the strength I need." (Philippians 4:13)

Have you ever been told by some well meaning person that there is something you can't do? Often the motive is to lessen the blow of what they think is the reality. They don't want you discouraged or hurt, so they tell you not to expect too much out of life because of your disability. Maybe not exactly in those words, but that's the point. To them, this may seem to be good advice, but it isn't.

I have known many people with disabilities who had been told that they couldn't attend college, couldn't work, and shouldn't look forward to a career, having a family, etc. I was told by a relative when I was a little girl that I'd never be able to work. Little did they know that God has given all of us a "can do" spirit that is alive and well, an inner strength which enables us to do and be all things in life.

In Paul's letter to the Philippians he says "I can do everything with the help of Christ who gives me the strength I need." God has given all of us inner strength. You can't get this kind of strength from going to the gym or buying a fitness machine. This strength moves us to press on when others tell us we can't. This strength moves us to go forward with our hopes and dreams when others tell us not to bother. This strength holds up our "can do" spirit and enables us to prove them wrong and God right time and time again.

Prayer: *Dear God, Help me to find the inner strength you've given me to press toward the life goals set before me.*

Persevering in the Midst of Uncontrollable Circumstances – Day 3

"…My gracious favor is all you need. My power works best in your weakness." (2 Corinthians 12:9)

On my way home from work one day I caught site of a small brown rabbit hopping through the tall grass that borders the expressway. In spite of the dangers surrounding this little furry being, it seemed content to hop about, probably searching for food. In the midst of speeding cars and fast moving 18-wheelers this beautiful little creature, caught in the middle of circumstances over which he has no control, is getting on with its life and doing what's necessary to survive.

Not far from where I live is a vacant lot where a gas station and car repair shop once serviced the neighborhood. Though there's a fence around it, garbage still finds its way over the fence to take its place among the weeds that have broken through the concrete ground. I noticed that there are sprays of very small and pretty white flowers, growing in the midst of the garbage and weeds. These tiny little flowers, growing up in the middle of circumstances over which they have no control, are persevering, determined to provide beauty to this ugly piece of land.

I think about those of us who have a disability, how far we've come in spite of our limitations. In the middle of our struggle with disability, we attend college, build careers, marry, divorce, raise children, run businesses, compete in sports, and the list goes on. In the midst of circumstances over which we have no control, we persevere, we get on with life.

Prayer: *Dear God, Though I have no control over what my body can't do, I thank you for what I can do. I thank you for the life, the abilities, and the gifts you've given me. Thank you for the grace you've shown me, the power you've demonstrated through me, and for enabling me to persevere in the midst of my disability.*

The Purpose God Sees in Us – Day 4

"… People judge by outward appearance, but the Lord looks at a person's thoughts and intentions." (1 Samuel 16:7)

In my home it's a real struggle to keep a usable drinking cup in the bathroom. Disposable cups seem to disappear, ending up lost somewhere in the house. After much frustration of trying to keep a drinking cup in the bathroom I gave up, until one day I opened a plastic container of frozen orange juice. I was about to toss the container when I took a second look at it and thought, this would make a nice drinking cup. Since I was going to toss it anyway, why not get a little use out of it before it disappears like the others. That plastic juice container which was destined for the trash stayed in the bathroom over a year. It lasted where decorative paper and plastic cups failed. It's a mystery to me, but it fulfilled a good and useful purpose.

I often liken those of us with disabilities to that plastic orange juice container. Our disability is not attractive and at first glance, it looks like we don't have a useful purpose. But unlike that juice container, God didn't have to take a second look at us to determine whether or not we could serve a useful purpose. In our disability is still purpose - God's purpose. People with disabilities are fulfilling God's purpose… he shows his power through us. Consider entertainers, actors, politicians and countless other people with disabilities, some we know and most we'll never know. In the midst of their disability, they're fulfilling the purpose God intended for them.

God sees a purpose in us even when others don't. God's purpose in us enables us to live full, productive lives. In God's purpose there is no fear of being tossed aside.

Prayer: *Dear God, I am thankful that you didn't have to take a second look to determine my purpose. Move others to help in fulfilling your purpose for me and for them as you intended.*

The Journey... Through Weakness and Into Strength – Day 5

"My gracious favor is all you need. My power works best in your weakness." (2 Corinthians 12:8)

Every now and then circumstances require me to take public transportation. The buses and trains are wheelchair accessible, and it only takes a few minutes for the driver to operate the lift to get me on and off. As I ride, I observe other people as they travel about. There are all races of people, senior citizens, middle aged folks, teens, children, and disabled, even some who are clearly dealing with mental illness. In my observation I often wonder what their journey has been. What has happened in their life that's brought them this far. What hurdles have they overcome?

All of us have journeyed through life, encountering one obstacle after another. For those of us living with disability, our journey is never a constant, even road. There are successes, and failures; good health and daily pain; medicines that work, medicines that don't, medicines with side effects so severe that often times you'd rather just deal with the illness. Like everyone else, we get up each day and prepare ourselves for another day's journey. We struggle to get out of bed, and deal with the physical, mental and emotional challenges of another day in a body that doesn't work like it should. But you know what? For most of us with lifelong disability, we instinctively embark on this journey everyday – it's a way of life. We just get up and do it!

However, no matter how natural it's become, no matter how independent we are, no matter how good the meds make us feel and move there is still that desire to have this thorn removed. The Apostle Paul felt the same way when he begged the Lord three different times to remove the thorn in his flesh. Each time, the Lord's reply to him was "My gracious favor is all you need. My power works best in your weakness."

Prayer: *Dear God, Thank you for the fine example you enabled the Apostle Paul to set before us. Thank you for showing us the same gracious favor you showed Paul and using our weaknesses to demonstrate your love and power.*

ADA... In God's Plan – Day 6

"And you, my child...will go on before the Lord to prepare the way for him..." (Luke 1:76)

The Americans with Disabilities Act (*ADA) has done for people with disabilities what Civil Rights legislation has done for minorities. It has opened up the door to equal opportunity and fair treatment for people with disabilities. ADA legislation is now over 20 years old, and can you believe there are still people who don't know what it is or what it's about -- perhaps because right now in their life, they don't have a need for its benefits, not yet. Benefits such as a wheelchair accessible building, a talking elevator with Braille floor buttons, or closed captioned news and movies for the hearing impaired.

I am so thankful that we have a God who looked into the future and built a solution to the problems facing people with disabilities. When Adam and Eve sinned in the Garden of Eden, God immediately began planning for the arrival of a Savior to redeem us from sin. Later he foretold the birth of John the Baptist who would come to prepare the way for the coming of Jesus. Though long in coming, ADA legislation has made a world of difference in the lives of millions of Americans with disabilities.

Prayer: Dear God, Thank you for the ADA law that was passed to protect people with disabilities from discrimination in employment, education, and housing; that requires buildings, transportation, communications, and technology to be accessible for those with disabilities. Thank you for seeing the ability in us. Never let us take it for granted.

*To learn more about the Americans with Disabilities Act visit: ADA.gov

The Cure All for All – Day 7

"I wait for the Lord… and in his word I put my hope."
(Psalm 130:5)

How many of us are hoping in medical science to come up with a cure that would enable us to be disability free. Are we to wait on medical science or is there a hope somewhere else we should be counting on?

Take polio for example. In 1952 there were an estimated 60,000 cases of poliomyelitis with more than 3,000 deaths in the United States with children being the most vulnerable. In 1952 Dr. Jonas Saulk developed a successful vaccine using a combination of viruses. Now virtually eradicated in the US since 1979, immunizations against polio are required by law. However, in countries like Nigeria and Sudan, polio is still claiming victims. According to internet sources, there are six countries where polio continues to infect people.

Let's talk about another hope. This hope is a cure for all, not just for some. This hope is found in Jesus Christ and can be learned about in God's word. The Bible is full of accounts of how Jesus cured sick people. Jesus came to cure a sin sick world. All disabilities are a result of inherited sin. It is only through Jesus' shed blood that disabilities will someday be a thing of the past because sin will be a thing of the past.

I am happy about the achievements of medical science. It's a relief to know that because of their immunizations; my daughter and granddaughters are protected from polio, measles, and mumps just to name a few. But they're not protected from everything. As a result of sin, we are still vulnerable to illness and disease. It seems as soon as one disease is fixed another pops up. When will it end?

We need something we can depend on, a hope in something that will wipe it all away. We need to hope in something that doesn't need to be tested in lab rats or monkeys before its used on humans. Though I respect and support the achievements of medical science, my hope and trust is in the One who has a cure for all.

Prayer: *Dear God, Thank you for the hope we have in Jesus of one day living a disability free life. Thank you for the researchers and scientist who diligently work to develop treatments and cures for people with disabilities. Thank you that their efforts are not in vein, but help us to endure as we wait on the fulfillment of your promises. And God, please move the governments of other countries to make vaccines and treatments available for its citizens as they are your children too and are also waiting on the fulfillment of your promises.*

God Sees the Heart – Day 8

"…The LORD does not look at the things man looks at. Man looks at the outward appearance, but the LORD looks at the heart."
(1 Samuel 16:7)

The Hunchback of Notre Dame long considered a horror story is everything but a horror story. This classic tale, written in 1831 by Victor Hugo, one of the most outstanding writers of the 19th century, is a masterpiece that touches the heart. The Hunchback of Notre Dame is the story of Quasimodo, a man born with severe physical deformities who is forced to live a life of abuse, neglect and loneliness in a world of medieval superstitions, oppressive government, poverty, and religious ignorance. Because the people think of Quasimodo as a monster, fear and ridicule is their normal response to him.

After viewing the movie version many times and finally reading the book I began to sympathize with Quasimodo. He endured abuse from his care taker and was told that the people only wanted to make fun of him. He was told to stay in the Cathedral, safe from the humiliation of their insults. Quasimodo didn't want safety, he wanted understanding and acceptance. Quasimodo would spend his life in the tower unless the attitude of the people changed and their fears replaced by understanding and knowledge. The attitude of the people is the real horror in this story.

Quasimodo is often described as "the deformed bell-ringer," "the piteous Hunchback," and so on. Neither of these descriptions reveals his true character and abilities. On the other hand the story reveals an inner person, capable and worthy of being loved and accepted. Quasimodo is kind and gentle with normal feelings and desires. You can see the inner man through his interaction with Esmeralda, the gypsy girl, after he saves her from execution. However, the people miss learning this about him because they won't let go of their fear of his outward appearance.

Prayer: *Dear God, Thank you that you can see my inner self and know my abilities and my strengths. I thank you that you have taken time to know me since before I was conceived. Please move others to see beyond my physical appearance and reach out to know me as well. Thank you and bless those who have done so already.*

Cracks in the Sidewalk – Day 9

"…God is faithful; he will not let you be tempted beyond what you can bear. But when you are tempted, he will also provide a way out so that you can stand up under it." (1 Corinthians 10:13)

Sidewalks like many streets are full of pot holes, cracks and uneven surfaces. As a wheelchair user, I roll over the bumpy sidewalks everyday going to and from. Sometimes I have to really maneuver my chair to avoid the rough spots. As I roll about the city, alongside and behind people who are walking, I often wonder if they notice the condition of the sidewalks. Do they ever feel the ground dip in one spot and rise in another?

Sometimes our walk with God can be like maneuvering the sidewalks and streets. We can be going along on a smooth surface and hit a rough spot that reminds us that we live in a sinful world. We need God's help to resist sin and avoid spiritual injury. Without God's help we cannot successfully avoid falling into sin. This is true for all, even for people with disabilities.

There are times when the desire to fit in, the longing for companionship, the want for a better physical life tugs and pulls on us with a vengeance. It is those times we are tempted to sin to get relief and have those desires met. When we give in, if relief comes, it's temporary. In a short while, the tugs and pulls start all over again. Its part of Satan's vicious plan to separate us from God.

The Apostle Paul tells us at that "No temptation has seized you except what is common to man. And God is faithful; he will not let you be tempted beyond what you can bear. But when you are tempted, he will also provide a way out so that you can stand up under it." (1 Corinthians 10:13) Paul says it's common to man, so even people without a disability have the same tug of war going on. But what is this "way out" Paul is talking about. The way out is only through Jesus.

Prayer: Dear God, In times when the desire to fit in, the longing for companionship, and the want for a better physical life engulfs me, thank you for providing a way out of the temptation to sin. Thank you for helping me realize that relief through sin is only temporary, but if I wait on you, you will give me the desires of my heart that are permanent.

Ice Chips – Day 10

"...but whoever drinks the water I give them will never thirst.
Indeed the water I give them will become in them a spring of water
welling up to eternal life." (John 4:14)

When I was twelve years old, I had to have two spinal
surgeries to correct my curved spine (scoliosis). This was a
year-long process that I came through successfully. However,
during the weeks and months in a body cast, the future didn't
matter. I was concerned about the here and now, and my now
was miserable. My Mom kept telling me "It'll all turn out all
right." What did she know that I didn't? Well, at the time I
wasn't aware of her incredible faith.

Following the last surgery, my Mom was let into the recovery
room to be with me. When I awoke from the anesthesia, there
she was suited up in a surgical gown and cap. If you've ever
had surgery where you are put to sleep with anesthesia, in
addition to some pain, you wake up with an unbelievable
thirst. Your mouth is dry and all you can think of gulping
down as much water as you can to quench the thirst. That's
how I felt when I woke up. My Mom was standing over me
with a cup of ice chips. I was begging for water, and she's
feeding me ice chips. I asked her why I couldn't have some
water. She said that the water would make me sick so the
doctor suggested giving me the ice chips instead. I was in too
much pain to argue so I ate the ice chips. She was right, later
in the day when the anesthesia had worn off; I was able to
drink some water.

Those ice chips weren't what I wanted, but it was what I needed at the time. As much as I wanted to drink a big cup of cold water, it would have been a mistake. I believe we still get fed ice chips when we really want water. Sometimes the wheelchair is what we have to use even though we really want to walk. Walking may expose our bodies to more stress than it's capable of handling. Perhaps we want to stop the medication because we feel fine. But skipping the meds could cause the re-surfacing of a condition the meds were controlling. What are your ice chips?

Prayer: *Dear God, Thank you for the ice chips you feed me every day...whether it's the wheelchair that relieves the stress on my body or the medication that keeps my condition under control. Above all thank you for Jesus' the living water that gives me spiritual healing and strength enabling me to make it through each day.*

Your Walk – Day 11

"… what does the LORD require of you? To act justly and to love mercy and to walk humbly with your God." (Micah 6:8)

Have you ever watched how people walk to see if you can see their personality in the way they move their arms, legs and feet when they walk. Years ago I had a friend who had what I call the authoritative walk. She walked very fast and sure, didn't shuffle her feet. Her steps were very strong and deliberate. I know a man who swings his arms when he walks, and his head bobs from side to side. When I see him, I think of a boy who is happy, but has a little mischief on his mind.

Closer to home, my daughter walks exactly like my oldest sister, with her head up and shoulders back. Do you ever wonder about your own walk? How would your feet move, would it be fast and strong, or slow and deliberate. Would your arms swing, would your head bob from side to side? If you've been disabled for a long time, it probably doesn't matter anymore. But what does matter is how are you walking in Jesus? Are we loving others as Christ loves us; showing forgiveness for wrongs committed against us; living a life of service to others; studying God's word and learning to apply it in our lives. This is the walk God requires us to have. It's not a physical walk, it's a spiritual walk.

Prayer: *Dear God, Thank you that because of your love for me I can walk with you. Thank you that this spiritual walk does not require legs that work, it only requires an obedient spirit.*

Never Without the Spirit Within – Day 12

"... I have filled him with the Spirit of God, with wisdom, with understanding, with knowledge and with all kinds of skills."
(Exodus 31: 2, 3)

There was a story on cable TV about a young girl who continues to excel in spite of being born without arms. She writes, types, cooks, and practices karate. There was another story on the internet about a young man in China who is also without arms. He plays beautiful classical piano with his feet. These are just two of countless stories of people with disabilities living a life of courage and perseverance under what appears to be difficult physical circumstances.

This brings me to the point of this devotional. People with disabilities who live a life without arms, legs, sight, hearing, and other abilities, live with courage and perseverance. We don't sit around having pity parties. We have a spirit within that is whole, complete, not lacking anything. It is the spirit of the living God that motivates us to pursue life in spite of physical challenges.

In spite of being without limbs or other natural physical abilities, we bring honor and praise to God with what we have. The Apostle Paul at says "... your bodies are temples of the Holy Spirit, who is in you, whom you have received from God? You are not your own; you were bought at a price. Therefore honor God with your bodies." Paul also tells us that we can do all this through Jesus Christ who gives us strength.

Prayer: *Dear God, Thank you for not withholding your sprit from us. It is your spirit within us which enables us to live life and pursue our dreams. It is your spirit within us that keeps us from pitying ourselves, but rather it encourages and moves us to bring glory and honor to your name.*

A Special Child for Special Needs – Day 13

"For God so loved the world that he gave his one and only Son, that whoever believes in him shall not perish but have eternal life." (John 3:16)

At a memorial service for a high school friend who passed away, family and friends got up to share their memories of Ed. Some of the memories were funny, others serious, and others familiar. What struck me were the familiar memories that his sister spoke about.

Ed's sister mentioned that when they were growing up, she used to resent him because it seemed he got all the attention. You see, Ed had a disability. He was the special needs child among his brothers and sisters. I was also the special needs child among my brothers and sisters. After we grew up, one of my brothers confided in me that he used to resent me because he felt I got all the attention. I didn't want that attention and hated being the center of attraction. Perhaps my classmate Ed felt the same way.

We're all special needs children, not just the child with the disability. Our need was so special and God loved us so much that he sent his special child, his son to save his special needs children. Sin is that great disability, that special need all of us have. Paul writes "for all have sinned and fall short of the glory of God (Romans 3:23)." So it's not just those of us with disabilities that have a special need, but it's all of mankind. Disability is the result of sin. Sin has God's attention because it hurts his children and hinders their relationship with him.

Paul also writes "For there is no difference between Jew and Gentile—the same Lord is Lord of all and richly blesses all who call on him, for, everyone who calls on the name of the Lord will be saved." (Romans 10:12-13) Even though God does not show special treatment, his son Jesus healed those with disabilities when he encountered them (Mark 1:34; 2:4). Since God does not show favoritism and he blesses all those who call on his name, even those with disabilities, we don't have to worry about being resented for being the center of his attention. So tell anyone who thinks you get too much attention that there is room in the center of God's love for all.

Prayer: *Dear God, Thank you for the attention you bestow on us. Thank you for sending your special son to heal your special needs children. Thank you that your love and healing power is for everyone, not just those with disabilities.*

Don't Leave Home Without Him – Day 14

"… I am always with you; you hold me by my right hand. You guide me with your counsel…" (Psalm 73: 23, 24)

The public transportation system in Chicago has special seating for people with disabilities. Riders are asked to surrender these seats when a senior citizen or person with a disability boards. There is a sign that says "Yield to seniors and people with disabilities." Have you ever thought about leaving home without your disability? It's like that popular credit card that we're advised not to leave home without. However, unlike that credit card, we don't have the option to leave home without it.

Disability is a part of us; it's woven throughout our limbs. We couldn't leave home without it no more than we could leave home without skin. Though your disability creates limitations you wouldn't wish on your worst enemy, it doesn't identify what you are or who you are. We are created in the image of God (Genesis 1:27).

Yes, I'd like to leave home without my disability, and I know that in God's due time, healing will come and I'll have that opportunity. In the meantime, I'll take my disability with me, everywhere I go. I'll also take along the One in whose image I am created, the One to whom I belong. In Psalm 103, David shares with us how God forgave him, healed him, even rescued him from death. I would never want to leave home without the One who could do all that for me.

Prayer: *Dear God, Thank you for being the One who has filled my life with good things, things no posted signs could ever bring about. Thank you for being the greatest advocate for people with disabilities.*

The Presence of God – Day 15

"You make known to me the path of life; you will fill me with joy in your presence, with eternal pleasures at your right hand."
(Psalm 16:11)

I always try to remind myself what life would be like without the presence of God in it. I'm sure it would be full of stuff that might make death a welcome friend. But when Christ entered the world to take away our sin, He also came to make his very presence move us to rejoice. To rejoice in the knowledge that he is able to make and is making life better.

When I was twelve and had come out of surgery my Mom was allowed into the recovery room. It's not easy to get into such places if you're not on the medical team, but somehow my Mom got in. When I woke up and saw her face, the pain was so much more bearable. She visited me everyday. Her presence made me feel better. That's how God's presence should be in our lives. Just knowing that if we call out to him, he'll hear us and is ready and willing to come to our aid is enough to get me through the anxieties of the day. The presence of God is powerful and available to everyone. Ask God into your heart, feel his presence, and get ready for a life worth living.

Prayer: *Dear God, Through your presence, help me to have a life that is worth living.*

A Question of Faith – Day 16

"Dear brothers and sisters, when troubles come your way, consider it an opportunity for great joy. For you know that when your faith is tested, your endurance has a chance to grow. So let it grow, for when your endurance is fully developed, you will be perfect and complete, needing nothing." (James 1:2-4)

Have you ever encountered someone, usually another Christian who tells you flat out "If you have faith you can be healed." I have, more than once. The last time was just a few weeks ago in a shoe store. This time I refused to let this person assume that because I'm disabled, I don't have any faith and that I don't believe in God's healing power. Though I very much appreciated her interest and concern, it was important for me to clear the misunderstanding that some able bodied Christians have about Christians who are disabled.

I shared with her my testimony of faith. Though I'm not healed physically, God has healed me spiritually. Like the Apostle Paul, God has not removed my thorn, but he has demonstrated his power in my life. Physical healing is what we desire, but not always what we need. God gives us what we need and promises to satisfy the desires of our heart.

There are many, many disabled Christians who have rich, rewarding and faith filled lives in spite of their disabilities. No matter the size of their faith, Christian with disabilities exercise it 24/7. It is our faith that enables us to endure the everyday trials that come with disability. Living a life of disability isn't easy, but we "Walk by faith and not by sight."

If you have taken the time to read this devotional, that is proof that God is showing a healing presence in your life as well. Don't let anyone assume that because you have a disability that your faith is weak or non-existent.

Prayer: *Dear God, Thank you for giving us a testimony that we can share with those who believe we have no faith. Through our testimony we demonstrate that we believe in your healing power. Thank you for your healing presence in our lives and help us not to make assumptions about the faith of others.*

Where Is The Thanks – Day 17

"He fell to the ground at Jesus' feet, thanking him for what he had done… Jesus asked, "Didn't I heal ten men? Where are the other nine? Has no one returned to give glory to God except this foreigner?" (Luke 17:16-18)

Sometimes being disabled has its perks when it comes to getting help for things like opening doors, reaching something that's high on a shelf, picking up something off the floor, carrying some heavy or cumbersome object. For the most part, people are always very helpful and I appreciate it more than they will ever know. I always say thank you for some kindness shown to me. This happens throughout the day every day.

I never tire of saying thank you to someone who has done something for me. Sometimes I even say it twice "Thank you, thank you!" God also wants us to be thankful to him for what he's done in our lives. In Luke, chapter 17, while Jesus was on his way to Jerusalem, he encounters ten lepers. When they see him coming into the town, they call out to him "Jesus, Master, have mercy on us! Jesus looked at them and told them to go and show themselves to the priest. As they went to do as Jesus instructed, their leprosy disappeared. Jesus made a point to notice that of the ten, only one returned to say thank you and to give him glory and honor for what he had done.

Acknowledging the goodness of others is so very important. It not only lets them know how much they are appreciated, but it also moves them to continue doing acts of kindness to others. But to acknowledge the goodness of God is extremely important. Giving God thanks for his blessings in our lives is part of our worship. Our thankfulness brings glory and honor to his name. We are to let our lives overflow with thanksgiving for all he has done (Colossians 2:7).

The next time someone opens a door for you or assist you in some way, make sure to tell that person "Thank You" and then give thanks to God who may have sent that person to help you at that moment in time.

Prayer: *Dear God, Thank you for all that you have done and will do for me. And when I am in need of assistance please send someone to help me and never let me forget to say thank you.*

Waiting in Faith – Day 18

Faith is the confidence that what we hope for will actually happen; it gives us assurance about things we cannot see. (Hebrew 11:1)

"God blesses the people who patiently endure testing. Afterward they will receive the crown of life that God has promised to those who love him." (James 1:12)

Living with a disability requires so much more patience than most people can imagine. We have to wait on our bodies to do what we need them to do, we have to wait on help from others, we have to wait on doctor appointments and decisions, medical test and results, wait on medication to stop the pain or clear an infection, we have to wait on the government, and the waiting goes on and on. We wait on healing.

For some of us, the wait on healing is short, and for others it last a lifetime. How long have you waited for healing? How is it possible to wait for a healing that may not come until after our departure from this earth? It is the sustaining power of faith in God's promises that helps us endure the wait and still enjoy life while daily thanking and praising God for his blessings.

The eleventh chapter of Hebrews talks about people who had great faith. It talks about how their faith helped them to please God, motivated them to do things at God's command without knowing any of the details of who, what, when, where or why. Moses wasn't a good speaker but he trusted that God was with him so he went to Pharaoh many times. In the end, Moses' faith in the promises of God enabled him to lead the Israelites out of Egypt. He trusted in God's promise that their future life would be better. God's word assures us that there is a blessing coming to those who patiently endure.

Prayer: *Dear God, Help me to be patient in my circumstances and to know that you are in control, and in your time, you will bring healing. I will continue to trust in your promise of a better physical life ahead. Thank you for giving me patience to carry on the wait and for showing us that there is no better alternative than to wait in faith with full expectation of the fulfillment of your promises.*

I Shall Trust and Not Worry - Day 19

My flesh and my heart may fail, but God is the strength of my heart and my portion forever. (Psalm 73:26)

Just when you think you have mastered how to maneuver through life and finally get your disability to somewhat of a manageable level your body starts to develop new ailments. Let's see, there's post polio syndrome, diabetes, hypertension, arthritis, pressure sores, and for some, the list goes on and on. Every doctor's visit is overshadowed by the fear of being told something else has developed. Every unfamiliar twinge anywhere in the body set's off a fire storm of new concerns. You say to yourself, Awe come on, what's next?

What's the alternative? Either I can make myself sick with worry or continue to trust God? Here is an excerpt from WebMD on the dangers of excessive worry.

"Are you an excessive worrier? Perhaps you subconsciously think that if you "worry enough," you can prevent bad things from happening. But the fact is worrying can affect the body in ways that may surprise you. When worrying becomes excessive, it can lead to feelings of high anxiety and even cause you to be physically ill. Chronic worrying affects your daily life so much that it interferes with your appetite, lifestyle habits, relationships, sleep, and job performance." (WebMD.com)

In other words, if I worry too much about what's going on with my body, I can really make things worse. Don't misunderstand what I mean about worry. It's right to be concerned about our bodies and to seek out medical advice and treatment when we suspect something out of the ordinary is going on. But in addition to seeking medical help, seek out God and ask him to help you not to worry excessively. *"So do not fear, for I am with you; do not be dismayed, for I am your*

God. I will strengthen you and help you; I will uphold you with my righteous right hand. (Isaiah 41:10)"

Prayer: *Dear God, My body is again showing signs of weakness. Ailments are coming at me from all directions. Just when I overcome one, another swiftly comes along. But you oh God are my sustenance. You have brought me this far and I trust you to take me even further. Strengthen me and help me continue on. Help me to remember your powerful promises of a future full of good health.*

You Need My Help – Day 20

A person's steps are directed by the LORD. How then can anyone understand their own way?
(Proverbs 20:24)

" LORD, I know that people's lives are not their own; it is not for them to direct their steps. (Jeremiah 10:23)

I'm sure you've turned down offers of help from people. I have. Perhaps it was to open a door or retrieve an item from a shelf. Sometimes the help is needed other times it isn't. But have you ever turned down help then discovered you actually needed it.

One time a woman offered to help me carry an item and I turned her down. A few seconds later, I dropped it. It was her remark to me that inspired this devotional. In a rather smug way she said "You see… You do need my help." In other words she was telling me "You're not as independent as you think you are." I said thank you and we went our separate ways.

None of us are as independent as we try to be. The physical challenge of getting to and from, carrying stuff, moving stuff often is a daunting task. Several times I've said to people, you know what? On second thought I do need a hand. Then I get the help I thought I didn't need.

Turning down help from people is okay if we actually think we have the situation under control. And if you see that you really do need help, don't be ashamed to go back and ask for it. But how often do we think we don't need God's help. At one time or another all of us were guilty of living as if we didn't need God's help.

In Mark 10:25 it says "It is easier for a camel to go through a needles eye then for a rich man to enter the Kingdom of God." I believe riches are not always material possessions and financial wealth. Riches can also mean rich in physical abilities, tip top health. For example, athletes are rich in good health. Even people with disabilities can have a degree of richness to their health. Those who are rich in good health may have an attitude that says "You know what, I can do this, and I can do that. I don't need anything or anybody to help me." That is dangerous thinking. Adam and Eve let Satan deceive them into thinking they didn't need God's help. That kind of thinking caused them to disobey God which catapulted mankind into a life of sin and death. (Genesis 3)

God's help can come as a helping hand from another person or it can be a wheelchair. It can be a new medication or a modified home with a ramp or chair lift. It can be spiritual with a small voice that says you need to pray more or study the Bible word more. In the midst of a life with disability, we still need to humble ourselves and accept God's help.

Prayer: *Dear God, Though I am thankful for my abilities let me always remember that I can do nothing without your help.*

God Sees Us – Day 21

Your eyes saw my unformed body; all the days ordained for me were written in your book before one of them came to be. (Psalm 139:16)

Some times sitting low in a wheelchair is a disadvantage because I tend to be out of the main line of vision for people who are walking or behind counters. Every now and then it's a little funny when I'm next in line and the cashier can only see the person standing behind me and says with some frustration "Next in line!" and the person behind me doesn't move. When I roll up to the counter I get the usual line "I'm sorry, I didn't see you down there." On more than one occasion I've had to maneuver my chair to avoid someone who was about to walk directly into me because he or she is staring straight ahead or talking on a cell phone and not taking the time to glance down. Folks don't always mean to overlook us, it just happens because they're looking at their eye level, not ours. It isn't a huge problem, but it is annoying.

There are times though when we are intentionally overlooked. On a conference call with a group of people who are disabled, one person who is visually impaired shared how he was advised not to attend a training session. His manager thought he wouldn't benefit from the session. He felt the manager was disregarding his professional need to attend that class. Another person on the call expressed how her request for an office was ignored. You see, she has some deafness and uses a hearing aid. When she does use the phone, she must use the speaker phone which is quite loud. Having an office where she can close the door would enable her to use the speakerphone in her work without disturbing her co-workers. In spite of the Americans with Disabilities Act we still struggle to get acknowledgement and fair treatment.

In Luke 13: 10-13 Jesus healed a woman who had been disabled for 18 years. The scripture doesn't say why she was at the temple, but it clearly shows that Jesus took notice of her and gave her healing. He acknowledged her presence, observed her condition, and took immediate positive action to help her. God looks down all the time. The Bible says that God looked so far that his eyes saw even the embryo of me (Psalms 139:16).

Prayer: *Dear God, Thank you for looking down from your throne of grace to see me, for acknowledging my presence and meeting my needs.*

"I can do everything with the help of Christ

who gives me the strength I need."

(Philippians 4:13)

www.ingramcontent.com/pod-product-compliance
Lightning Source LLC
Chambersburg PA
CBHW030309030426
42337CB00012B/643